ROMA

MW01200372

Story Structure for Romance Novels

GWEN HAYES

Romancing the Beat: Story Structure for Romance Novels

Stock art Dollar Photo club

Edited by FWS Media

First Printing, 2016

Print ISBN-13: 978-1530838615

Ebook ISBN: 978-1519990723

https://www.facebook.com/romancingthebeat/[1]

https://www.romancingthebeat.com

---

1. https://www.facebook.com/romancingthebeat/

Table of Contents

Welcome

HI, I'M GWEN.

I write kissing books.

I am also a freelance editor. My clients write kissing books.

Guess what I read for fun? Kissing books.

But I also read a lot of craft books: writing, story structure, how to outline, how to write with no outline, how to write dialogue that sparkles, how to create a bomb with a bale of hay, a stick of gum, and a—okay...that I made up. (Though my job does include looking up some things that some might consider shady.) But the point is, I am forever reading books about how to do what I do only *way moar better*. And boy am I grateful for those books. But while I was saving the cat and sending my protagonist on a heroine's journey and writing screenplays that sell, I noticed that while a lot of the advice was so spot on it made me excited to stop reading and start writing, something was still missing.

These structure books don't exactly nail the romance arc.

Romance has two heroes, not one. Romance has genre expectations. Romance has story beats that need to be hit before it can be called a kissing book. But not the same ones, or exactly the same ones, as that hero saving a cat on his journey to selling a screenplay. (These are all wonderful books, by the way. I highly recommend reading *Save the Cat* by Blake Snyder, *The Writer's Journey: Mythic Structure for Writers* by Christopher Vogler, and *Writing Screenplays that Sell* by Michael Hauge.)

And so I wrote the book I needed to read. And the one I needed to tell my clients about.

I have a sort of recipe that I share with my clients. When something is nagging them about their book, it's usually because they left out one of the ingredients. Since we're talking about books not cake, we'll call them story beats even though they are more like ingredients. Beats, in this case, are ways to measure movement of a story for pacing and content. Just like *ta-ta-tee-tee-ta* moves music. (Shout out to elementary school music teachers!)

The following story beats are intended to help you craft the romance arc that will hook your reader and keep them on the line all the way to a satisfying ending. This book is *especially* helpful for category romance and romance novellas, which are often treated like they are the same as single title, but they are not. The romance beats will need to be braided with your external plot if you write longer, complicated titles, especially romantic suspense.

And never fear. This book does not discriminate against your chosen writing process. Pantsers, plotters, plantsers, plontsers...however you identify yourself, you are welcome here.

Also, I'm often...irreverent. And I quote pop culture, relying heavily on movies like *Mean Girls* and Taylor Swift songs and internet memes. Reading this book is going to be like hanging out with me on Twitter.

If you are interested in a cheat sheet to help you as you go along, I have created one for my Romancing the Beatniks community. When you sign up, one of the perks is an 11-page PDF that you can print and fill in as you read. For more information, please visit here[2]:

---

2. https://facebook.us15.list-manage.com/
   subscribe?u=24925851985f905a5857cdb3c&id=7638692b2e

What is What

WHAT THIS BOOK IS:

This guide is for a very specific niche. I don't go into depth about all the elements of great storytelling or story structure. I am going to delve only into the specifics of the internal/romance arc for romance novels, which is especially helpful for those who write shorter stories and category length.

- A new tool for your writer's toolbox.
- A road map of the romantic journey your characters take in order to earn their happy ending by facing their biggest fears.
- A vehicle for me to drop '80s references.
- No, seriously. This book is littered with them.

Who this book is for:

- Romance writers who have been told their books focus too much on the external plot.

- Romance writers who know something is missing from their book, but are not sure where to look to find it.
- Non-romance writers looking to strengthen the romantic elements of a different genre book.

Why I wrote this book:

- It's the first step in my world domination plan. I'm saving the world...one love story at a time.

Theme

BEFORE WE GET INTO the actual beats, let's talk about theme. Many authors tell stories in order to explore themes of importance to them and maybe even persuade the reader to consider those ideals. Some just write stories and let the scholars of the future deduce theme from their works. I'm not concerned with the other themes. You are writing a romance, so your theme is already picked out for you.

Love Conquers All

In a broad sense, *all* romance books are about one theme: Love conquers all.

Romance readers have genre expectations just like any other genre. The biggest of those expectations is the HEA (happily ever after) or the HFN (happy for now). If love doesn't conquer all at the end of your story, you didn't write a romance. You might have a great story with romantic elements, but if your characters don't have a happy resolution, then you need to find a different shelf for your finished book to live on. That's not a bad thing; it's just not a romance thing.

You can and should write whatever kind of book you want to, just be careful what you call it. If you ordered a chocolate cake, but when you take a bite it's yellow cake because the baker wanted to do something "edgy," you'd feel betrayed. That's how romance readers feel when they buy a romance that doesn't end happily.

Don't betray your readers.

Back to the theme because I can feel some of you getting frothy. I'm not saying your book is *only* about love conquers all. Many, many romance writers also gravitate towards secondary or tangent themes. You may write a few books and realize that redemption seems to come up time and again for your characters, for instance, and that is great. Fabulous. Don't ever change. But the main theme you will explore in every romance book you write is love conquers all. And what's also great about that is you know how your book will end before you even start.

So...love conquers all. That's pretty broad. Your job, in your story, is to show two examples of "all," assuming you are writing about two protagonists falling in love. If you have three or more, you have more work than the rest of us. But have fun!

So what does love conquer in *your* book? A long-held-onto shame? A fear of intimacy? A failed marriage? Low self-esteem? Trust issues? Lonely Starbucks lovers? I mean a long list of ex-lovers? (*See, I told you...Taylor Swift song AND internet meme.)

Your characters each show themselves to you and the reader with a gaping hole in the place their hearts should be. At the end of your book, they go from hole-hearted to whole-hearted via love conquering all.

That journey from hole-hearted to whole-hearted is the romance arc for each character. The plot of your book is what you throw at them by way of obstacles that encourage them to confront that hole.

It is possible that one of your characters *does* want to go all in with the other from the very beginning. He or she may relentlessly pursue the other and you might think that means you don't need to give them a hole-hearted-to-whole-hearted arc, but you'd be wrong.

There is still something holding him or her back, it's just going to be a subtler transition than the other protagonist. Something has kept him or her from being his or her best self. Perhaps they are jumping into wanting a relationship with the other character too soon—they are in love with love. Maybe they are destined mates and biologically drawn to the other by a force bigger than themselves, but don't let them off the hook there. They still need to fall in love via their human heart, not just the werewolf/ bear/ lion/ dragon/ vampire fated mate heart. Perhaps your hero is pursuing the heroine because he wants to take her to bed, but doesn't realize he's also going to have to fall in love. What I'm saying in a lot of words is this: both characters should have an arc devoted to change deep within, whether or not one of them appears to already be on board.

Whatever is keeping your characters from falling in love, being in love, or thinking they deserve love is what your book is going to be *about*. All your plot points and beats need to be looked at through the lens of that fear or misconception or deep-seated issue. Your book needs to show the process your protagonists endure to change so that by the end of the book they are able to give their whole heart to someone else and accept love in return.

If you don't mind, I'd appreciate it if you would please re-read that last paragraph. I'll make it easy for you: Whatever is keeping your characters from falling in love, being in love, or thinking they deserve love is what your book is going to be *about*. All your plot points and beats need to be looked at through the lens of that fear or misconception or deep-seated issue. Your book needs to show the process your protagonists endure to change so that by the end of the book they are able to give their whole heart to someone else and accept love in return.

This issue, fear, or misconception is also often referred to as a character flaw or wound. It's that tender spot or hole in their hearts that they protect at all costs. They have likely spent years or their entire lives living with that hole. When an animal is injured, it will often lash out at those trying to help. Your characters are going to feel a primal instinct to protect the holes in their hearts like they would a raw wound. They have built walls around their hearts, adopted masks or personas to hide them, and will react with ferocity to keep others out.

Lucky you. You get to poke the bear.

An Aside About External Plot

THE DEPTH OF THE EXTERNAL plot arc in the story you tell will depend a lot on the length and the sub-genre of your romance. For instance, a mystery or romantic suspense needs to weave in a complicated and often action-packed subplot and a villain, whereas a category length romance has less room for more than one subplot. Notice I called the external element a subplot. Your *main* plot is hole-hearted to whole-hearted. (My goal is to inflict a giant earworm on you by the end of this book. If you are singing "Hole Hearted" by Extreme at any time during your reading, I win.)

Focusing on the romance arc does not excuse you from having an external plot altogether, though. I prefer to frame this plotline as external goals. What do your characters want? This might change as the book goes on, but they should always have an agenda, and if you want a page turner, it should conflict with the external goal of the other main character.

Examples of how external goals change: Dorothy wants to run away from the farm, and then spends the rest of the movie trying to get back to it. Luke wants to join the academy, and then he wants to save the princess, and then he wants to blow up the Death Star.

Examples of conflicting external goals in romance: Hero wants a historical home his grandfather built to be saved from the wrecking ball; Heroine wants the promotion that comes with breaking ground on the high-rise so she can afford to put her sister in a private school for the deaf. Neither one of the characters is wrong or immoral—they just want different things.

You will also have a premise—the thing that makes everyone go all one-clicky on your book when they read the book description—and it usually includes tropes. Don't give me side-eye. Tropes in romance are a lovely thing. Tropes, familiar and common plot devices used in storytelling, make the romance world go around. Fly your trope flags high, writers.

This book does not go into great depth about the external subplot—but you want one that makes a reader say, "Take my money," when they read your back cover copy. The external goals in conflict are what make for great copy or book description, so you don't want to skimp here. External goals make your chosen trope and premise unique and interesting. But you will want to braid this subplot into the romance arc, not the other way around.

The back of your book will not talk about the romance arc as a selling point—that's your external goal/premise/trope real estate. Inside the book, your characters' inner journeys from unable to accept love to unable to stop themselves from falling in love is what clutches your readers in their own hearts.

A Structure in Four Phases

THREE ACTS. NO, FOUR Acts. No, it's a Pyramid. No, it's...

Most storytelling is done in three acts: beginning, middle, and end. That's why the three-act structure is something discussed a lot in structure books and blog posts.

Cool. We got that out of the way.

I also like to split the middle into two parts when I'm *thinking* about a story, whether before I write it or when I am editing a client's book. Why? Because it feels less daunting to me to eat the elephant in smaller chunks.

That's gross.

But like the saying goes: How do you eat an elephant? One bite at a time.

I'm not reinventing the storytelling wheel; I'm just making sure I'm not overwhelmed with 50% of an elephant sitting in front of me all at once.

So, I split the three acts into four phases. A nice manageable elephant, if you will.

Set up

Falling in love

Retreating from love

Fighting for love

These four phases have five beats I want to hit. Sometimes this means one beat per scene, but sometimes several beats appear in the same scene. It's a recipe, not a preflight checklist. There is room for variation.

The glory of the beats is that you can use this system before you write, as you write, or after you write. You can use it while you revise, and as a special bonus, to draft a quick synopsis.

But wait there's more.

If you want to use a beat sheet as an outline, you can start from anywhere on it and work from what you already know about the book that's been percolating in your head toward the abyss of what is yet undiscovered.

But wait there's more.

If you are writing a short story, novella, or category length romance, you could be done when you get these beats eaten. Um...written.

And if you act today, no one will make you eat an elephant.

Beat Sheet

SO, WHAT IS A BEAT sheet? For me, it's a Scrivener file with each story beat written on an index card. (Scrivener is writing software that I adore. I'll link in the Appendix.) For you, it might be a sheet of paper with each beat listed on it. Or 20 3x5 cards. Or 20 pieces of paper. Or a Word document. Or something you keep in your head as a mental checklist. Whatever works for you.

Here's our master list:

(H1 and H2 designate gender-neutral protagonists.)

Set Up

- Intro H1
- Intro H2
- Meet Cute
- No Way 1
- Adhesion Plot Thrust

Falling in Love

- No Way 2
- Inkling this could work
  - Deepening desire
- Maybe this will work
- Midpoint of LOVE Plot Thrust

Retreating from Love

- Inkling of doubt
- Deepening doubt
  - Retreat
  - Shields up
  - Break Up

Fighting for Love

- Dark night of the Soul
  - Wake-up/Catharsis
  - Grand Gesture
- What whole hearted looks like
  - Epilogue

You're probably thinking of an arc that looks like a rainbow, but when I think of the romance arc, I see a caduceus. A caduceus looks like this:

EACH OF THE SERPENTS is a protagonist, and the rod they wrap around is love. (It sounds like I'm telling a dirty joke, but I'm not)

In my own version of the caduceus, at each story beat, the protagonists circle each other once around that rod, then back away to their respective corners. But each twist brings them closer together because they don't have enough slack to get all the way back to where they started from. Their old self isn't the same, but neither is their new self.

So shall we begin?

Where to Start?

FOR THE SAKE OF SIMPLICITY, this book will sometimes refer to your protagonists as H1 and H2. One is not more important than the other and the H is gender neutral. The beats are the same whether your characters are gay or straight. The beats are also the same if your book is sweet or erotic or something in between. The beats stay the same if your romance is paranormal or historical or comedic or angst-filled.

Sometimes your book starts in your head with a character who won't stop talking to you. Sometimes it's a premise or a trope you want to explore. Sometimes it's a great ending. If you are plotting/outlining your story, you can start anywhere you want on the beat sheet so long as you know the flaw/wound/fear/hole of both H1 and H2. And again, these beats don't care if you use them before, during, or after your drafting stage. Or all three.

If you are writing a short story, novella, or category romance, you might want to start with the trope. For instance, if you love amnesia stories, and who doesn't, you might start there and find characters who fit the trope.

The following chapters are going to go into more detail about the list of beats. If you are writing a short work, you might be able to just do one beat per scene and be done. If you are writing a complex or longer book, you might find you write some of the beats more than once and sometimes beats are combined in a scene. It's all good. You just want to make sure you hit every one of these beats.

And yes, Virginia, you can even write the beats out of order if you want to. You're the writer; you can do what you want. But some of them build on each other and your pacing might suffer. If you have a good editor, he or she will tell you all about it. But carry on.

I usually start with what I call a spark sheet, which is basically a bunch of rambles of everything I know about a story before I start to write it. Lots of it changes or never comes to fruition, but it's what sparked me to begin. There are no rules to a spark sheet. You can handwrite, dictate, type in Comic sans...it's just downloading your brain. (Don't use Comic Sans, though, I was kidding about that. There is a rule.)

After I have downloaded my brain to the spark sheet, I might try to organize it: Characters, plot points, things to research, etc. Then I start at the beginning of my beat sheet and see which ones I know. So let's check out the beats.

Phase One: The Setup

WELCOME TO THE FIRST act and the first phase of the beat sheet. The next five beats are setup and should bring you to about the 20-25% mark. The objective is to introduce the characters, the world, the premise, and the romance arc. (Though we know it's really a romance caduceus.)

Just because we call it a setup, don't be fooled that you can take your time and show a character just waking up to start her day (cliché) yawning and all alone. A nice juicy whiff of trouble is necessary from the very beginning. You want to show their normal, everyday life, yes. But you want to show that it is already about to change.

Even if you plot out of order, the one thing you must know is your character's flaw/wound/misconception about love. Don't proceed without it. Remember, everything in your book is seen through the lens of the wounds of your characters.

Introducing H1 and H2—Two beats one chapter

'80S SOUNDTRACK FOR THE Intro Beat:

"Don't Stop Believin'" by Journey

"I Wanna Dance with Somebody" by Whitney Houston

"In the Air Tonight" by Phil Collins

"Dancing in the Dark" by Bruce Springsteen

YOUR INTRODUCTION TO one of your first main characters sets the tone for your novel. This beat is important. Again, you might not start here in your planning process, but when you get to here, this is the deal.

We'll be looking at H1 and H2 together in this chapter, but they are actually two different beats in your story. Their purpose is the same, however. I prefer to see two different scenes, one after the other, for these two beats. You're the writer, though. You do what you want.

Objectives for H1 and H2 introductions:

Introduce protagonist in a way that makes that character compelling.

Notice I did not say likable. A character does not have to be likable. They *do* have to be compelling. Compelling means the reader wants to root for your heroes. Anti-heroes are often very popular and fun to read and write. Many current romance heroes are so over-the-top alpha male they are referred to as alphaholes...but some readers LOVE them.

Possible ways to make a character compelling: character is best at what he or she does (we humans like successful people), character is humorous, character is suffering through undeserved misfortune (sympathetic), character is highly driven, character shows a selfless act, character loves something or someone more than themselves, character is going through something the reader can empathize with....

Show your character's slice of life but throw a hitch in it.

Give the reader a good look at what normal is, but make sure there is some kind of trouble or something unexpected in the middle of it. Gone are the days when you can meander through detail after detail of the setting before readers meet your first protagonist. Effective storytelling means giving the reader someone to root for quickly, then showing us the details through that character's point of view. But this slice of life is brief before we smell a whiff of trouble.

*Do yourself a favor and don't start with your character alone and thinking. That is a temptation for backstory info dump. Nobody likes backstory info dump. They won't like it in the rain or on a train or with a fox or in a box. I promise.

GIVE OR INTRODUCE YOUR character's external goal.

This goal may not be the Big Plot of your story. But it's something they want or *think* they want. Give that goal some stakes, too.

Bonus points if the external goals of H1 and H2 are in opposition.

Introduce or hint at what your character needs.

What is holding him or her back from being whole-hearted and being able to give and accept love? You may not reveal in great depth the flaw/wound/issue at this time, because again, nobody wants to read a bunch of backstory info dump. (I am serious about this Sam-I-Am.) But you need to hint that the *last* thing this person wants is to meet the love of his or her life right now. In fact, H1 might not even know that he or she is unhappy. But you need to show the reader that something is missing and that something is H2.

I know that I said you only need to hint at this inner hole at this time, but please don't misunderstand the importance of this character flaw. *Every* scene in your romance is informed by your character's wound—even the ones not part of the romance arc. Every single one of them. So while you are hinting at the issue here, that doesn't mean it's not the driving force of your book.

On page the character hints at a deeper issue. Off page that issue is everything.

So, if your whole book is your character overcoming this deep-seated fear, it's up to you to make sure you have crafted a backstory that is worthy. A breakup in the past, in and of itself, is not a worthy character wound. That breakup needs to have a deeper resonance. His ex-wife cheated on him? Meh. His ex-wife cheated on him with his once beloved brother? Better. His ex-wife cheated on him much the same way his mother cheated on his father before she left and never came back? I'm seeing possibilities.

Meet Cute

'80S SOUNDTRACK FOR MEET Cute Beat:

"The Way You Make Me Feel" by Michael Jackson

"Kickstart my Heart" by Mötley Crüe

"Head Over Heels" by The Go-Gos

THE MEET CUTE, A TERM that has been around since the 1940s, is when the H1 and H2 meet for the first time. It can also be referred to as the inciting incident, though not everyone is in agreement about that. The word *cute* insinuates a light or comedic factor, but that may not resonate for your book. You do want it to be memorable. If they already know each other, that's okay. This is the first time they are *on page* together.

Sparks should fly.

The POV character will likely have some internal thoughts regarding the attractiveness of the other. How attracted they are will depend on your tone, genre, and heat level. Erotic romance characters will likely have more torrid first impressions than those in a sweet romance. A comedic book will have a funny meet. An enemies to lovers story might have a very angsty scene. Or a funny one. You're the chef, you decide.

A well-crafted meet cute will showcase how the external goals and internal flaws introduced in the Intro beats are in conflict.

The POV (point of view) character will have an initial physical reaction and an emotional reaction of "not for me."

The meet cute should reflect the tone of your story. It sets up how the two characters will go on for a time. Use all the senses in this beat, and pay attention to detail. After all, your characters are going to tell the story of how they met to their grandchildren someday. Make it memorable for them.

No Way #1

'80S SOUNDTRACK FOR NO Way Beat:

"What's Love Got to Do with It?" by Tina Turner

"Fire and Ice" by Pat Benatar

"I'm Alright" by Kenny Loggins

THE FIRST NO WAY BEAT is the argument your character voices against falling in love. It sets up the romance arc for the reader. The character basically says, either out loud or in internal dialogue, the reason that he or she *will not* fall in love. Not now, not ever, but especially with the character from the Meet Cute.

You can add more of the backstory here—not too much, don't make me pull out more Dr. Seuss—but give the reader more on the page about why the last thing the character wants is to fall in love, therefore the last thing the character wants is to give in to the attraction felt in the Meet Cute. No way, no how.

Sometimes, especially in sexier books, a character *does* want to pursue the physical attraction. That character still needs to argue against the transformation you are planning on putting him or her through. For instance, an example of this would be the familiar trope about characters who decide they can sleep together once to get this attraction "out of their systems." They assume this will be a one-time thing and then they can go back to their regular lives and the nursing of their cold, deadened hearts. We know they will transform, and they will figure it out eventually.

You are going to challenge the No Way Beat—this belief the character has—for the rest of the book, so start that arc now. Give it voice and give it legs. You might have one beat for H1 or H2 here, and then the other in Phase Two. Or you might have POV scenes for each in this area in which they iterate their particular disdain for love.

I suggest making it clear and on page. Think of Shakespeare's famous quote, "The lady doth protest too much."

Adhesion

'80S SOUNDTRACK FOR ADHESION Beat:

"Stuck on You" by Lionel Ritchie

"Be Near Me" by The Thompson Twins

"Love is a Battlefield" by Pat Benatar

SO YOUR CHARACTERS have met. They've expressed their non-interest in falling in love, generally, and with the other character, specifically. Or they have expressed their interest in having a fling and getting it out of their systems. If they had their way, they would be done at this point.

But then the book would be done, and we just started.

The next beat is Adhesion. The story needs to be crafted in a way that neither of them can walk away from the other. This is where a lot of tropes are introduced: marriage of convenience, going on the run, hiding from the bad guys, pretend relationships, stranded in a snowstorm, entered into a contest or battle together, forced into a partnership. This beat pushes you into the second act. It's a plot thrust. They cannot walk away from the other now. Not until they see this conundrum through.

It's at this time in your book that you might also introduce an additional external goal or goals for your characters. Their whiffs of trouble have come and gone, and now they are adhered to each other like glue. Your external goal may have something to do with the trope or the sub-genre you are writing.

They are stuck. The door to the first phase, Act I, closes firmly behind them.

It's time for you to rub your hands together gleefully and set about making them miserable.

Phase Two: Falling in Love

WE JUST GOT THROUGH the set up phase and are at about 20-25% of the book.

Now begins the falling in love phase. This is where I see a lot of romance books falter. *You* know the two are meant to be together forever, but you have to *show* your reader the same, even if H1 and H2 are oblivious. I see way too many authors forget to write the scenes that endear the couple to the reader. If this were a movie or a soap opera, Phase Two chapters would be the scenes in a montage shown when the hero is sure he's lost his love near the end of the show.

In Blake Snyder's, *Saving the Cat*, he would call this section "Fun and Games."

During this phase, our characters are still going to proclaim their unwillingness to change, but it's your job to start shooting holes in the walls they have built around their hearts. The reader will see they are clearly made for each other. Your characters might not for a while. Each scene needs to build on the sexual tension—whether or not you consummate that tension on page, it's still there.

They are also going to be doing a two-steps forward/one-step back dance in this phase. Brainstorm several scenes showing them getting closer and then backing away. Later, when they are lamenting their losses, the most important thing your characters will take away from this phase is that being with the other character made him or her a better person. Not just a horny person. A **better** person. The person they could be if they were whole-hearted instead of hole-hearted.

If you are hearing from your beta readers or reviews that they don't believe the progression to the I-love-yous at the end, go back to this section and make sure you have shown H1 and H2 getting to know each other. Even if they are enemies, it's here they find things to like or respect about the other.

No Way #2

'80S SOUNDTRACK FOR NO Way 2 Beat:

"Faith" by George Michael

"Danger Zone" by Kenny Loggins

FOR THE NEXT 25% OR so of the book, you the author are going to attack the argument voiced against transformation in the No Way Beat from the last phase. In this beat, however, you should restate the argument. This means you are going to make sure the characters are still positive that they are right about love and their reasons for not falling into it.

If you only had a No Way Beat for one character, this is the place for the other to express disdain for opening their heart. Feel free to employ more bits of backstory. This beat is about your characters gathering their ammo and girding their loins as they are now stuck with the other character and want to avoid temptation, but don't forget to tempt them.

If you had No Way Beats for both of them in the first phase, just restate them. I'm not suggesting that you rehash word-for-word. But a subtle nod to the reason they are unable to love or be loved with perhaps another hint of why is good here.

The Inkling

'80S SOUNDTRACK FOR INKLING Beat:

"Straight Up" by Paula Abdul

"Somebody Like You" by .38 Special

"Leave a Tender Moment Alone" by Billy Joel

THE INKLING BEAT IS where you begin to have some fun!

Whatever is going on in your external/trope driven plot, remember your focus is attacking your character's false belief about what he or she stated in either No Way Beat 1 or No Way Beat 2. We're going to escalate our attacks, but for now, let's give one or both of them a hole in that wall they have erected around their hearts. Something needs to make them stop and think.

Possible ways to do that include: an intimate moment (measured by heat level of your book), witnessing a good deed carried out by the other protagonist, witnessing the other do something that doesn't mesh with the way the character has been characterized in your protagonist's head, a tender moment, sexy moment, fun moment, sharing personal truths or secrets, defending the other physically or emotionally, something sets them up as "us against the world" for the scene, a kindness is paid.

Deepening Desire

'80S SOUNDTRACK FOR DESIRE Beat:

"Take My Breath Away" by Berlin

"Wishing Well" by Terrence Trent Darby

"Crazy for You" by Madonna

YOUR CHARACTERS ARE now embroiled in the business of falling for each other. You've shown them an inkling of what could be if they were whole-hearted instead of hole-hearted, but they are still reticent. They may also have a murder mystery to solve at this time, or maybe a villain has twisted his mustache and caused havoc, but let's get a beat in the romance arc about desire.

This is definitely a two steps forward scene. They can no longer deny to themselves that they physically want the other. The heat level of your book will determine if they act on the desire in a physical way. Inside the characters' heads, though, they are feeling drawn in a way that's hard to fight.

You'll want to make sure you have long, lingering gazes and plenty of visceral reactions from here on out, but don't forget the sweet moments. This is a romance. They are falling in love, not just lust. They are starting to show each other glimpses of who they really are.

Maybe This Time

'80S SOUNDTRACK FOR THE Maybe Beat:

"I Want Your Sex" by George Michael

"This Could be the Night" by Loverboy

"Let's Go All the Way" by Sly Fox

In the screenwriting world, they say "sex at sixty." Meaning: they have sexual relations on page 60 of a script. It's the halfway mark in a two-hour movie. You're writing a book and page numbers are not as confining, but *nearing* the 50% mark, where we are now, is a good time to ramp up the desire for the last beat.

If your book has no sex at all, think: true intimacy. If you write sex and they haven't had it yet, now is a perfect time, right before the midpoint. Up to now, they have been showing each other things that make them vulnerable to the other and it's turning out okay, right? (For now.) What if they gave in to that temptation?

This beat is called Maybe because you have now attacked your characters' "No Way Beats" enough that they are beginning to wonder what it would be like to let go of the fear holding them back. They can see that maybe they have been wrong. Maybe love isn't so bad. And they'd really like to get naked now.

If your characters have already had sex before this point, by all means let them have it again. But make sure it's different. More intimate. They need to be more vulnerable by the end of this beat.

Midpoint of Love

'80S SOUNDTRACK FOR MIDPOINT of Love Beat:

"Waiting for a Girl Like You" by Foreigner

"Save a Prayer" by Duran Duran

"Almost Paradise" by Mike Reno and Ann Wilson

The midpoint. You're halfway through. Your characters are like Charlie Brown running to that football, and Love has promised not to yank it away at the last minute again. This is the beat where you show them everything they want and it's in reach. They may not be ready for I-love-yous, but they have opened the gates on their fiercely guarded hearts.

Maybe they have a perfect morning after their Maybe Beat sex the night before. Maybe they open up in a way they haven't yet. Maybe they tell someone, a friend or confidant, about how right it feels. Maybe they just internally think that this might be it.

Bring them really, really high here. It's a false high, but they don't know that. Everything is better than they thought it could ever be.

They are holding on to a helium balloon. You are holding on to a pin.

Phase Three: Retreating from Love

ONE THING ABOUT THAT last beat: it was a false high.

Bummer, right?

They don't get to be happy-ever-after until all the walls come down, not just an open gate, and they walk through fire and open themselves up to love. They are figuring out now that they *can* love, they might even be starting to admit it to themselves that they are feeling it. Woohoo! But humans are stubborn to change, and the change they need has to come from facing their flaws/ wounds/ misconceptions and overcoming them.

How does a caterpillar become a butterfly? He doesn't blink and get wings. He has to bust out of that cocoon. That nice warm, safe cocoon.

Your protagonists have to bust through the walls around their hearts and they are going to be reluctant to commit fully to that. It's your job to push them. Begin your attack and specifically target their soft spots.

Look back at your No Way Beats and start exploiting. Does he think all women cheat? Does she think all men leave? Does she think she can't have love and a career because her mother gave up hers to raise a family? Does he think he is a failure at responsibility because he should have saved his buddy during battle but couldn't? Whatever their issues are, that's what you're going to hit them with in this phase. You're going to want to be easy on those poor little dears, but don't. If you set up Phase Two with enough compelling reasons to give love a try, they'll come back to those in the end.

Inkling of Doubt

'80S SOUNDTRACK FOR INKLING of Doubt Beat:

"Can't Fight This Feeling" by REO Speedwagon

"Take On Me" by A-Ha

Things feel pretty good for your protagonists right now, at least in regard to their relationship arc. The external plot you cook up might not feel great for them, but they just had their false high moment with the other and they are beginning to allow for the idea that they can fall for someone else. They probably don't want to admit it, but they can see a different path and it's not as bad as they thought.

Except now you're going to give them each a quick sucker punch right in the feels.

Go back to your No Way Beats and give them an inkling of doubt custom made for their hole-hearted selves.

Each beat in this phase will get progressively harder on them, so maybe think of the worst thing that could happen first and then level down four different beats.

For this one, just remind them of their wound/flaw. They might shove the thought away quickly, but plant the seed of doubt.

Deepening Doubt

'80S SOUNDTRACK FOR DEEPENING Doubt Beat:

"With or Without You" by U2

"What About Love" by Heart

THEY ARE REALLY STARTING to get attached now. The intimacy is continuing or may even appear to be growing, but the seed of doubt you planted in the last beat just poked up through the ground.

Your characters are not going to admit to each other that anything is wrong, but of course the other will be feeling a little reticence, thus causing them to feel a little more guarded as well. They might still be doing the horizontal mambo, but when their heartbeats return to normal, they have some internal dilemma.

Again, you might have more than one scene for this or any beat. They might get progressively worse until the next beat.

Retreat! Retreat!

'80S SOUNDTRACK FOR THE Retreat Beat:

"Harden My Heart" by Quarterflash

"Should've Known Better" by Richard Marx

EACH OF THESE BEATS has been bringing your characters two steps backward and one step forward again. Make sure your beats are tailored to their weaknesses. If she thinks all men leave, then she's going to be watching for signs of him leaving. And she's going to see signs that aren't there, so she'll be putting him on the defensive while she's also building boundaries to protect herself from his eventual departure. She won't understand that she's pushing him away, but your reader will. (Don't make this all about misunderstanding though. If she's seeing signs of him "leaving" he should also be showing signs, even if that's not his intent. Perhaps, he is keeping a secret from her about the external arc, so she is sensing something and attributes it to him closing down on her.)

The Retreat Beat is one where you leave subtext behind and let them actually say, either in internal or external dialogue, what they fear and that they are going to protect their hearts. They might not say it to each other because that would be too easy, wouldn't it? No, she might tell her mom or friend, or maybe she just tells herself.

Like the No Way Beat, you just want to make it clear. They are retreating in order to not get hurt.

Shields Up

'80S SOUNDTRACK FOR THE Shields Up Beat:

"Love Bites" by Def Leppard

"If You Leave" by OMD

"Goodbye to You" by Scandal

Well, here we go! Your heroes finally get to be right about something.

Whatever they foretold in their No Way Beats comes true. If all men leave: her lover leaves her. If all women cheat: he *thinks* he has proven that she is cheating. (She's not, of course. If she is, you didn't write a romance.)

It will be a couple of beats yet before they realize that they created this self-fulfilling prophecy. But for right now, let them bask in the glory of being right. So basically, the beats bookend themselves like this:

No Way Beat: I don't believe in love/will never love again/don't deserve love because_____.

Shields Up Beat: I knew better than to believe in love/love again/think I deserve love because when I let my guard down _____.

Break Up

'80S SOUNDTRACK FOR THE Break Up

"If Looks Could Kill" by Heart

"Blame it on the Rain" by Milli Vanilli

"Tainted Love" by Soft Cell

IT'S OVER. THEY POSSIBLY broke up in the last scene, and this is the reaction beat from the other character. Or perhaps this is the final blowout. What you want here, to make your point resonate, is for one or both of your characters to have a choice: choose love or choose fear. This is a major attack, and one or both of them have to *choose fear*.

They have to *choose* this. Too many romance novels have this moment, often called the black moment, be driven by an external plot point. She's trapped in a building and there is an explosion and everyone is sure she's dead—it's a very nice gut punch, but it's external.

If the black moment comes from external plot points, your heroes are not learning anything about themselves. If your black moment involves danger, make sure to tie it to an emotional beat. Did his first wife die because he couldn't protect her from his enemies? Has his fear all along been that he didn't want to get too close to the heroine because he carries guilt that he can't protect those he loves? Then when that explosion happens it should be because he sent her into that building when he pushed her away from him.

Always have your black moment be tied to the moment when your heroes choose to hold onto their fears/flaws/wounds/ misconceptions instead of opening their hearts completely. You can have your external black moment at the same time as your romance arc black moment/break up, but they have to be tied together by being hole-hearted.

Phase Four: Fighting for Love

WELCOME TO THE LAST phase of your romance arc. The following beats are all about your heroes realizing they are cotton-headed ninny-muggins and clawing their way back to each other using the footholds you gave them in the second phase. So hopefully you gave them some good ones!

Dark Night of the Soul

'80S SOUNDTRACK FOR DARK Night Beat:

"Don't Know What You've Got 'til it's Gone" by Cinderella

"Here I Go Again" by Whitesnake

"Promises in the Dark" by Pat Benatar

"Every Rose has its Thorn" by Poison

I didn't make up the term Dark Night of the Soul, but I love it. It's also metaphorical for "death of the ego" and "rock bottom." Basically, it's the place where your heroes think they should feel better than they do about the stupid thing they just did. Suddenly, they are staring out windows while montages of Phase Two play across their mind and every song they hear is about heartbreak. It's when they realize they did this thing to themselves.

Sometimes, this is where a mentor or friend tells them they are idiots. If your heroine is trapped in a building, your hero thinks she's dead and he's lost his chance to tell her he loves her.

Those poor lovesick souls are just about to wake up and smell the coffee, but give them a good scene in which to wallow. They have to know they chose this instead of what they wanted.

Wake Up! Smell the Coffee

'80S SOUNDTRACK FOR WAKE Up Beat

"What if I'd Been the One to Say Goodbye" by .38 Special

"The Flame" by Cheap Trick

"Separate Ways, Worlds Apart" by Journey

EVEN AFTER A DARK NIGHT, the sun rises.

It's a new day, and your heroes have spent some time realizing they are miserable because they chose to be miserable. They've had some advice, and now the clouds clear and they realize they will always be hole-hearted unless they destroy the wall around their fears/wounds/misconceptions.

And this beat is where they say: This time I choose love over fear.

Only it can't be that easy, can it? I mean, they probably broke each other's hearts. It's not like a phone call will fix it. (If it does, you need to add more conflict!)

They have to take off the armor and stand in front of each other defenseless. They have to choose to do this.

And at least one of them needs to go way out on a limb to woo the other back. That comes next!

So for this beat, let them wake up and know they have had the power all along to smash that wall around their hearts. Probably, one of them will have more smashing to do than the other.

They might also realize in this beat that they might be too late to win back the love they lost. But this is where they get the will to try.

Grand Gesture

'80S SOUNDTRACK FOR GRAND Gesture:

"In Your Eyes" by Peter Gabriel

You knew I was going to pick that song, didn't you? The iconic grand gesture of romance movies is Lloyd Dobler holding a boom box over his head and playing "In Your Eyes" to win back his lady. Other grand gestures you may be familiar with: Harry running all the way across town to tell Sally he loves her at midnight on New Year's Eve, Josie Geller standing on that baseball field waiting for her first kiss or public humiliation, Edward Lewis facing his fear of heights to kiss Vivian on the fire escape, Sandy and Danny giving up their old selves, and outfits, to fit into each other's worlds at the graduation carnival, Baby finally doing the leap, Pam walking across hot coals and then confessing her feelings to Jim, Crocodile Dundee surfing the crowd in the subway station to get that kiss, Jerry's "You complete me" in front of the angry divorce club, Jack staying with handcuffed Annie on a runaway subway instead of saving himself. The grand gesture is a fixture in romance, and when you sell it short, you miss out.

For the grand gesture to work and delight your reader, there needs to be risk. Your character has just had an epiphany and is ready to be courageous. He or she must be willing to put it all on the line now or risk losing the one thing they need to become whole-hearted. It's life or death now. And by death, I mean symbolic (death of career, death of pride, death of a goal or a dream) or literal death (hey Jack, sorry Rose couldn't scoot over and let you survive the sinking *Titanic*) depending on the tone and genre of your book.

Common gestures include: a race to the airport/across town/ somewhere with a ticking clock and lots of obstacles, public declaration with risk of humiliation, overcoming a specific fear (heights, snakes, children—this has to be a plot point earlier or it falls flat), literal risk of life, sacrificing a dream or a goal for the other to see his or her dream come true.

Play this beat up. It's the one that gets cheers in a theater. It's good to have at least one groveler, but both of your characters might need to perform a grand gesture (Danny and Sandy) if that's how your arc is working. They might even be at two different times. For instance, in *While You Were Sleeping*, Sandra Bullocks' character publicly confessed her feelings to Bill Pullman at her wedding to his brother, and then Bill Pullman's character brought his entire family to propose to her at the subway booth.

This beat is the moment your entire novel has been building to. Make it grand. Make it funny. Make it angsty. Make it whatever you want, but make it big.

Since this is a romance, this is also where they get their happy ending. You might draw it out a little—amp up the tension—but it's gotta end at some point with your own version of "You had me at hello."

Whole-hearted

'80S SOUNDTRACK FOR WHOLE-hearted:

"Open Arms" by Journey

"Reunited" by Peaches and Herb

"Heaven" by Warrant

The closing image, or denouement for all you classy lit majors, is a bookend of sorts that shows a good contrast of where your lovers were at in the beginning compared to where they end up. A nice mirror image of the Meet Cute is always appreciated. But any mirror moment will have some impact. Mirror their first kiss? An intimate joke? The setting of their first meet? A pivotal plot point from Phase Two?

They kissed and made up in the last beat, but show your reader what whole-hearted looks like for these two. You've put them through the wringer. This is your chance to make it up to them.

You may also go on to write an epilogue, or this might be the end. And the end sells your next book. You want that reader to have such an endorphin rush that they sprain their finger one-clicking their next read from you.

Epilogue

'

80s Soundtrack for the Epilogue:

"Time of my Life" by Bill Medley and Jennifer Warnes

"Nothing's Gonna Stop Us Now" by ~~Jefferson Airplane Jefferson Starship~~ Starship

An epilogue is fairly standard practice in a lot of romances. Your reader might be clinging to each page, not quite willing to submit to their upcoming book hangover yet. Some readers love sappy epilogues: weddings, babies, and a glimpse at a perfect life. That doesn't mean you have to bring out babies and white dresses, though, if you're not feeling it. A glimpse into the future is nice. A little interaction with characters for your sequel is also good.

One thing I caution writers about is that "too perfect" is boring. People are still the same people when they get their happy ever after, they are just happy. Don't turn your characters into cardboard at the last hurrah. Keep that spark that made them dance off the page. No personality transplants. If he was a scoundrel, he's still a scoundrel, just limited to one woman now. (And who doesn't need more scoundrels in their lives?) It's up to you, a master at your craft, to manage a scene with little conflict that is still intriguing.

Sample Beat Sheet

BELOW IS A SAMPLE OF the beat sheet for *Don't Stop Believing* by Gwen Hayes. It was a short story of 15k words, so the beats often happened one after the other in the same scene. Don't read this if you don't want spoilers!

It's not a pretty thing, this beat sheet. I wanted to share a working outline that helped me get the words on paper. It probably won't tempt you to one-click the book because...it's a shorthand outline. It's not meant for marketing. I didn't go into great detail. It's not a compelling read as is.

Again, if you don't plot beforehand, that is totally fine if your process works for you. Using the structure to map missing beats after your book is written works well. It's one of the editing tools that I use for my clients' books.

Set Up

Intro H1: Scene: Small town Main St, outside, two days before Christmas. H1: Grumpy lumberjack with a heart of gold. Wound=doesn't believe he is worthy of love. Scene: Needs to get supplies before the winter storm hits. Even though he tries to be a hermit, the townspeople obviously care about him. He agrees to foster a special needs puppy for one townsperson. Whiff of trouble: Needs to go to the library but doesn't want to see his secret crush, the new librarian.

Intro H2 and Meet Cute: Scene: Library. H2: Nerdy librarian looking to settle down and raise a family. Wound: Falls for the wrong kind of men—the kind who don't want the same things he does. His secret crush on the grumpy lumberjack is a prime example of wanting the wrong kind of man. Librarian flirts with lumberjack to tease him into flirting back. Lumberjack gets flustered. The storm is coming in and the librarian plans to leave town in the snow, despite lumberjack's warning. He doesn't want to be alone on Christmas.

No Way 1 and Adhesion: Scene: Driving down the icy road. Lumberjack reiterates to himself how he's better off alone. He is no good for anybody. Lumberjack comes across librarian in the ditch. They won't be able to get the car out tonight and they are further away from town than cabin, so he's going to have to bring librarian home with him to ride out the storm.

Falling in Love

No Way 2 and Inkling this could work: Scene: Rustic cabin. Lumberjack patches librarian up and serves him dinner, but as they share an intimate moment, lumberjack shuts down and pretends not to be attracted. He is too set in his ways and likes to be alone.

Deepening desire: Scene: Rustic cabin and woods. They spend the day getting a Christmas tree in the woods and decorating lumberjack's cabin, getting to know each other. (It is a Christmas novella, after all.)

Maybe this will work: Scene: In front of fireplace. Lumberjack shares the reason he left the Navy and became a recluse. They kiss, but lumberjack still feels too much self-loathing to pull librarian into his world.

Midpoint of LOVE Plot Thrust: Scene: Bedroom. They make love when librarian tempts lumberjack too much.

Retreating from Love

Inkling of doubt and Deepening doubt: Scene: Bedroom. Lumberjack pulls away the next morning, full of regret and knowing librarian is better off without him. He sneaks out to get librarian's car out of ditch so he can go home, leaving a note.

Retreat: Scene: Cabin. Librarian is hurt and realizes he shouldn't have pushed. Lumberjack isn't the guy for him. He's falling into the same pattern again—trying to make someone who doesn't want love fall in love with him.

Shields up and Break up: Scene: Cab of truck. Lumberjack and Librarian fight as they go back to town, each saying things to hurt the other. Librarian tries one last effort to kiss lumberjack, but lumberjack pulls away.

Lumberjack feels he was right about love—he doesn't deserve it. Librarian feels he was right about love—he doesn't know how to choose men who don't only want sex.

Fighting for Love

Dark night of the Soul: Scene: Cabin. Lumberjack looks around his house and sees librarian everywhere he looks. He realizes how cut off from the world he's made himself.

Wake-up/Catharsis: Scene: Cabin. Lumberjack takes a good hard look at his life and how he's been selfish and unseeing of all the good people around him. Instead of pushing them all away, he should have been grateful. He calls one of the townspeople, the one who finagled him into taking the special needs puppy, and asks for help getting librarian back. This shows he cares more about fixing things with librarian that keeping up his reclusive ways.

Grand Gesture: Scene: Town Center. Librarian is taken aback when lumberjack shows up at his door in a horse drawn carriage. Lumberjack takes him to a party he set up so librarian wouldn't be alone on Christmas (recall that is why he wanted to leave town despite blizzard warning—so he wouldn't be alone on Christmas—mirrors meet cute). Lumberjack confesses his feelings. Librarian reciprocates.

What whole-hearted looks like: Scene: Library two months later. (setting mirrors Meet Cute again). Lumberjack asks librarian to marry him. Librarian accepts.

Appendix

SUGGESTED READING LIST

Romance Your Brand by Zoe York

Writing Screenplays That Sell by Michael Hauge

Save the Cat by Blake Snyder

Save the Cat Writes a Novel by Jessica Brody

The Writers Journey: Mythic Structure For Writers by Christopher Vogler

Outlining your Novel by K.M. Weiland

GMC: Goals, Motivation, and Conflict by Debra Dixon

Helpful Things

Scrivener template for Romancing the Beat: https://www.romancingthebeat.com/free-stuff

Romancing the Beatniks Newsletter: https://www.romancingthebeat.com/sign-up (PDF cheat sheet)

About the Author

GWEN HAYES WRITES, edits, and reads kissing books. To keep in touch about her Romancing the Beat shenanigans, please visit the Facebook page[1] and/or sign up for the Romancing the Beatniks newsletter[2]. For editing services and courses, please visit www.romancingthebeat.com[3].

To find out more about her fiction for young adults and grown up readers, please find her at www.gwenhayes.com[4].

---

1. https://www.facebook.com/romancingthebeat/

2. https://www.romancingthebeat.com/sign-up

3. http://www.romancingthebeat.com

4. http://www.gwenhayes.com

Made in United States
Orlando, FL
07 December 2024